Scurry and Squeak

Bringing Home a Guinea Pig

by Amanda Doering Tourville

illustrated by Andi Carter

Special thanks to our advisers for their expertise:

Sharon Hurley, D.V.M.
New Ulm (Minnesota) Regional
Veterinary Center

Terry Flaherty, Ph.D.
Professor of English
Minnesota State University,
Mankato

PICTURE WINDOW BOOKS
Minneapolis, Minnesota

Editor: Jill Kalz
Designer: Hilary Wacholz
Page Production: Michelle Biedscheid
Art Director: Nathan Gassman
Associate Managing Editor: Christianne Jones
The illustrations in this book were created with mixed media.
Photo Credit: Eline Spek/Shutterstock, 23

Picture Window Books
151 Good Counsel Drive
P.O. Box 669
Mankato, MN 56002-0669
877-845-8392
www.picturewindowbooks.com

Library of Congress Cataloging-in-Publication Data
Tourville, Amanda Doering, 1980-
Scurry and squeak : bringing home a guinea pig /
by Amanda Doering Tourville ; illustrated by Andi Carter.
p. cm. – (Get a pet)
Includes index.
ISBN 978-1-4048-4859-7 (library binding)
1. Guinea pigs as pets—Juvenile literature. I. Carter, Andi,
1976-, ill. II. Title.
SF459.G9T68 2008
636.935'92–dc22   2008006429

Table of Contents

A New Guinea Pig. 4
Choosing a Guinea Pig. 6
Coming Home. 8
Time to Eat 10
Grooming 12
Keeping Clean. 14
Staying Healthy 16
Good Night, Guinea Pig! 18
A Happy Pet 21

Guinea Pig Close-up. 22
Guinea Pig Life Cycle. 23
Glossary 23
To Learn More 24
Index. 24

A New Guinea Pig

Terell is getting a pet guinea pig! What kind of guinea pig will he choose? Will it be a baby or an adult? What color will it be? Will it have long hair or short hair?

TIP
Long-haired guinea pigs need regular brushing and trimming. If you don't have time to groom your guinea pig, choose a medium- or short-haired guinea pig.

Having a guinea pig is a lot of fun, but it is also a lot of work. Is Terell ready?

Most Popular Guinea Pig Breeds
American (short hair)
Abyssinian (medium-length hair with tufts)
Peruvian (long hair)
Rex (short, frizzy hair)

Choosing a Guinea Pig

Terell is buying his guinea pig from a breeder. Some people buy guinea pigs from a pet store or animal shelter.

TIP

Guinea pigs are happiest around other guinea pigs. If you can, get two females or two males right away. Male and female guinea pigs should not live in the same cage. Guinea pigs bought at different times should not live in the same cage, either.

Terell makes sure the guinea pig he picks is healthy. A healthy guinea pig is active and curious. Its eyes are bright and clear. Its hair is clean and dry, with no bald patches. The animal should let someone hold it without too much fuss.

Terell names his new guinea pig Trixie.

Coming Home

Terell's new guinea pig is home! But she is a little scared. Everything is new to her. Terell puts her in her cage. He gives her a day or two to get used to the new place.

TIP
Guinea pigs like to hide when they play. Give your guinea pig cardboard boxes or tubes to hide in.

Terell talks softly to his guinea pig. He gives her a treat. Once she eats out of his hand, Terell picks her up. He holds her firmly against his chest with both hands. He makes sure to support her rump and back legs.

Time to Eat

Terell feeds his guinea pig special food he buys at a pet store. The food has vitamin C. Guinea pigs need vitamin C every day. Terell also feeds his guinea pig fruits and vegetables. An orange slice or a leaf of dark-green cabbage is a nice treat.

TIP
A guinea pig's front teeth never stop growing. Keep your pet's teeth from getting too long by giving her wood chews. You can find these at a pet store.

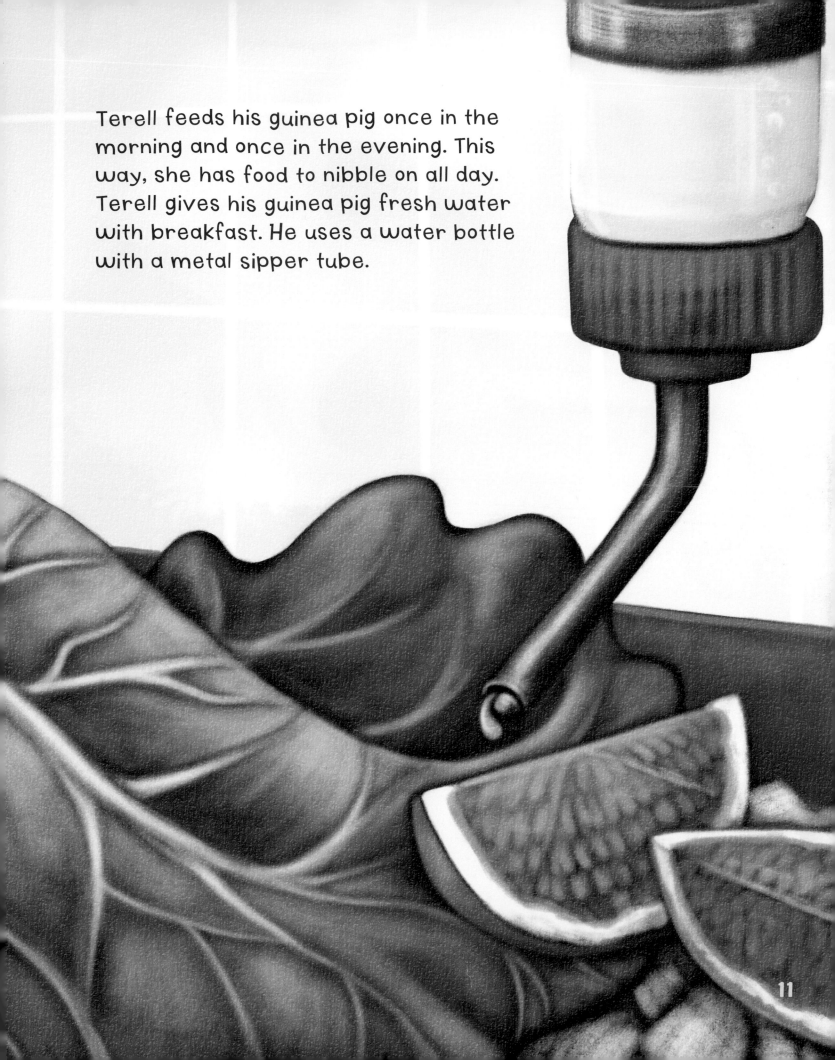

Terell feeds his guinea pig once in the morning and once in the evening. This way, she has food to nibble on all day. Terell gives his guinea pig fresh water with breakfast. He uses a water bottle with a metal sipper tube.

Grooming

Terell takes a shower each morning to clean up. But his guinea pig doesn't need to shower. She grooms herself. She licks or bites her hair and smoothes it with her front feet. Every three months, Terell helps his mom and dad bathe his guinea pig.

Terell gently brushes his guinea pig once a week. He uses a small brush from the pet store. His parents clip the guinea pig's claws once a month.

TIP
If you have a long-haired guinea pig, it is important to brush her every day. This keeps the hair from getting tangled. If your guinea pig's hair gets too long, ask an adult to trim it. You can also take your guinea pig to a pet groomer.

Keeping Clean

Terell cleans his guinea pig's cage at least once a week. First, he puts his guinea pig in an empty box. He asks his mom or dad to watch her. Then he scoops the dirty bedding out of the cage.

With a damp cloth and a stiff brush, Terell cleans the bottom and sides of the cage. He waits for the cage to dry. Then he puts in 2 to 3 inches (5 to 8 centimeters) of new bedding. Terell uses bedding made from recycled paper. Hay, aspen wood shavings, and crushed corn cobs also make good bedding.

TIP
Soap and other household cleaners can be harmful to your guinea pig. Pet stores sell pet-safe cleaners that you can use to clean your guinea pig's cage.

Staying Healthy

Guinea pigs need checkups just like people do. Shortly after getting his guinea pig, Terell takes her to the veterinarian. The vet answers all of Terell's questions about caring for his pet.

Once a week, Terell gives his guinea pig a checkup. He makes sure her eyes, nose, and ears are clean. He makes sure her claws aren't too long. He checks her hair for bald patches.

TIP
Guinea pigs and people can get sick from the same germs. Wash your hands before and after you hold your guinea pig to keep both of you healthy.

Good Night, Guinea Pig!

Terell keeps his guinea pig's cage in his room. The cage is away from doors and windows that could let in cold air.

TIP
Your parents may not want your guinea pig in your room. If so, make sure you put the cage in a place that is dark at night and light during the day. Keep it out of the sun and away from cold air.

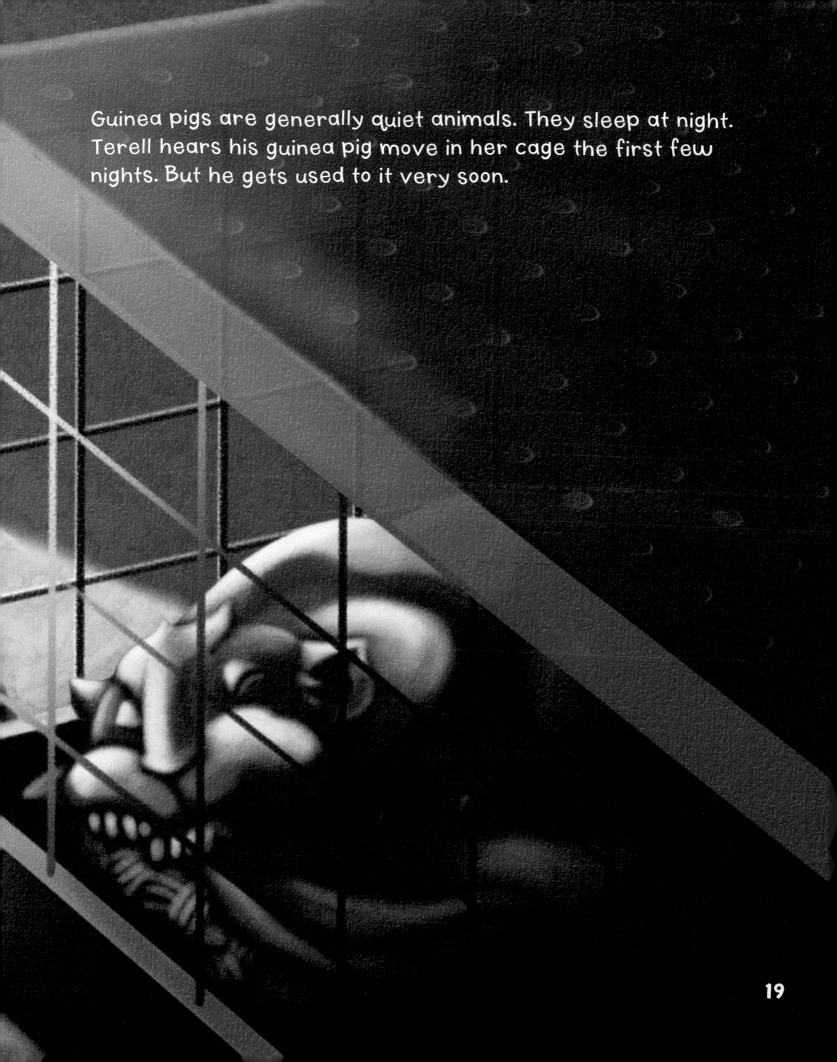

Guinea pigs are generally quiet animals. They sleep at night. Terell hears his guinea pig move in her cage the first few nights. But he gets used to it very soon.

A Happy Pet

Guinea pigs are great pets. Terell loves his new guinea pig and takes good care of her. Having a healthy, happy friend for five to eight years is worth the hard work!

Guinea Pig Close-up

A guinea pig's **EYES** are on the sides of its head. To see forward, the animal must turn its head.

A guinea pig's **EARS** can hear many sounds human ears can't.

WHISKERS help a guinea pig feel its way around and find food.

A guinea pig has no true **TAIL**, just a few small tail bones.

A guinea pig's **TEETH** never stop growing. But they are always being worn down by eating.

A guinea pig has four **TOES** on each front foot, but just three on each back foot.

Guinea Pig Life Cycle

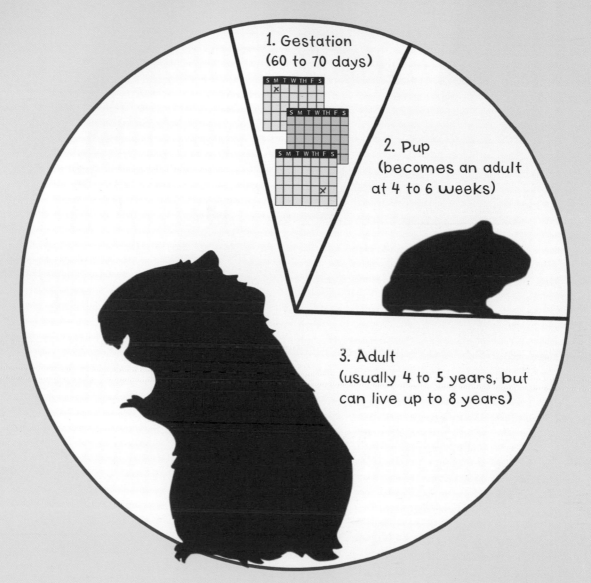

1. Gestation
(60 to 70 days)

2. Pup
(becomes an adult
at 4 to 6 weeks)

3. Adult
(usually 4 to 5 years, but
can live up to 8 years)

Glossary

animal shelter—a safe place where lost or homeless
pets can stay

bedding—materials used to make an animal's bed

breed—a kind or type

breeder—a person who raises animals to sell

gestation—the amount of time an unborn animal spends
inside its mother

groom—to clean and make an animal look neat

veterinarian—a doctor who takes care of animals; vet, for short

American Guinea Pig

To Learn More

More Books to Read

Foran, Jill. *Caring for Your Guinea Pig*. New York: Weigl Publishers, 2004.

Nelson, Robin. *Pet Guinea Pig*. Minneapolis: Lerner Publications, 2003.

Ross, Veronica. *My First Guinea Pig*. North Mankato, Minn.: Smart Apple Media, 2002.

On the Web

FactHound offers a safe, fun way to find Web sites related to topics in this book. All of the sites on FactHound have been researched by our staff.

1. Visit *www.facthound.com*
2. Type in this special code: 1404848592
3. Click on the FETCH IT button.

Your trusty FactHound will fetch the best sites for you!

Index

bedding, 14, 15
body parts, 7, 9, 10, 12, 13, 17, 22
breeds, 5
cage, 6, 8, 14, 15, 18, 19
choosing a guinea pig, 4, 5, 6
cleaning, 12, 14, 15
food, 9, 10, 11, 22

grooming, 4, 12, 13
hair, 4, 5, 7, 12, 13, 17
health, 7, 16, 17, 21
life cycle, 23
sleep, 19
veterinarian, 16
water, 11

Look for all of the books in the Get a Pet series:

Flutter and Float: Bringing Home Goldfish
Purr and Pounce: Bringing Home a Cat
Scurry and Squeak: Bringing Home a Guinea Pig
Skitter and Scoot: Bringing Home a Hamster
Twitter and Tweet: Bringing Home a Bird
Woof and Wag: Bringing Home a Dog